GOD ADDS HIS SUPER TO YOUR NATURAL TO PRODUCE THE SUPERNATURAL

Andrew Wommack

Published by Andrew Wommack Ministries, Inc.

Woodland Park, CO 80863

ISBN 13 TP: 978-1-59548-796-4
ISBN 13 eBook: 978-1-6675-1490-1

For Worldwide Distribution.

1 2 3 4 5 6 / 28 27 26 25

Contents

Would you like to get more out of this teaching?

Scan the QR code to access this teaching in video or audio formats to help you dive even deeper as you study.

Accessing the teaching this way will help you get even more out of this booklet.

awmi.net/browse

It's Not All God

The title of this booklet may seem strange, but it's one of the most established truths of the Bible. Every miracle in the Bible was dependent upon someone obeying the Lord and doing something in the natural before the miracle-working power of God became manifest through the supernatural. This is reflected in many scriptures, but here are just a few.

> *Now unto him that is able to do exceeding abundantly above all that we ask or think,* ***according to the power that worketh in us****.*
>
> Ephesians 3:20 (emphasis added)

> *And she went and did according to the saying of Elijah: and she, and he, and her house, did eat* many *days*
>
> 1 Kings 17:15

... faith, if it hath not works, is dead, being alone.

James 2:17

... faith without works is dead

James 2:20

Likewise, these next verses show that a lack of action was the reason many did not receive the supernatural manifestation of God's will for their lives.

Yea, they turned back and tempted God, and limited the Holy One of Israel.

Psalm 78:41

... If ye will not believe, surely ye shall not be established.

Isaiah 7:9

So we see that they could not enter in because of unbelief.

Hebrews 3:19

For unto us was the gospel preached, as well as unto them: but the word preached did not profit them, not being mixed with faith in them that heard it.

Hebrews 4:2

It's a fact: God's "super" needs our "natural" to produce the supernatural. Every miracle in the Bible occurred because someone took action, based on their faith in God. The Lord doesn't act "sovereignly," as the word is often used in religion today to say that He acts independently of us. Instead, the Lord has given every believer authority to act on His behalf. The Lord told us to resist the devil, and he would flee from us (James 4:7). He told us to speak to the mountain, and it would move. He didn't tell us to talk to Him and ask Him to move the mountain for us (Mark 11:23).

There are unlimited examples of this in the miraculous stories the Bible relates.

God's Provision Precedes Your Need

Take, for instance, the time Peter was asked if his master paid taxes.

> *And when they were come to Capernaum, they that received tribute* money *came to Peter, and said, Doth not your master pay tribute? He saith, Yes. And when he was come into the house, Jesus prevented him, saying, What thinkest thou, Simon? of whom do the kings of the earth take custom or tribute? of their own children, or of strangers? Peter saith unto him, Of strangers. Jesus saith unto him, Then are the children free. Notwithstanding, lest we should offend them, go thou to the sea, and cast an hook, and take up the fish that first cometh up; and when thou hast opened his mouth, thou shalt find a piece of money: that take, and give unto them for me and thee.*
>
> Matthew 17:24-27

Let's take a closer look at what happened here.

Before Peter could tell Jesus what he was thinking, Jesus revealed He already knew what had happened. That's supernatural. Jesus, as God, knows every thought in every heart (Ps. 139:1-4).

Then there was the coin. The Lord didn't create this coin—counterfeiting is against the law. Also, the Lord doesn't have money in heaven. He didn't drop this coin down from heaven. Money is a man-made product. Someone lost this coin in the sea. It was just something that happened naturally. But it was supernatural that Jesus knew of it and had a fish swallow the coin, which was the exact amount needed to pay the taxes for Peter and Himself.

Then Jesus supernaturally had that exact fish jump on the hook that Peter threw in the water. The scripture doesn't say that Peter baited the hook. Jesus just told him to cast a hook in the sea. It's possible Peter put bait on the hook, but it is for certain that it was the first fish Peter caught that would have the coin. That's not just a coincidence. That was supernatural.

But if Peter hadn't done his part in the natural, which was going fishing, the supernatural that the Lord wanted to do would not have manifested. It took a combination of the supernatural things Jesus knew and instructed Peter to do, along with the natural thing Peter did in obeying the Lord's instructions to produce this supply. If Peter had not gone fishing, all the supernatural things the Lord had orchestrated to meet this need would not have made any difference. The supply would have been in the fish's mouth, but Peter and Jesus would not have benefited from it.

A similar thing happened in Luke 5 when Jesus asked Peter if He could use his boat to move away from the shore a short distance so He could speak to the multitude. And the Lord didn't use Peter's boat without compensating him. After the sermon ended, Jesus told Peter to launch out into the deep and let down his nets for a catch. Jesus was going to pay Peter for the use of his boat by giving him a miraculous catch of fish.

Now when he had left speaking, he said unto Simon, Launch out into the deep, and let down your nets for a draught. And Simon answering said unto him, Master, we have toiled all the night, and have taken nothing: nevertheless at thy word I will let down the net.

Luke 5:4-5

Notice that Jesus told Peter to let down the nets, plural. However, Peter said he would let down the net, singular. We often limit God through partial obedience. If Peter had let down the nets, plural, he would have had an even greater catch and might not have broken his one net. However, if Peter had not obeyed and let down at least this one net, he wouldn't have caught any fish. He had to do something in the natural to receive this supernatural catch of fish.

Luke goes on to record the results of obeying the Lord's instructions.

And when they had this done, they inclosed a great multitude of fishes: and their *net brake. And they beckoned unto* their *partners, which were in the other ship, that they should come and help them. And they came, and filled both the ships, so that they began to sink.*

Luke 5:6-7

Everyone wants a net-breaking, boat-sinking catch, but they don't always do what they need to do to receive it. The Lord had commanded every fish in the sea to head for Peter's boat, but that wouldn't have made any difference if Peter hadn't provided some way to catch them. This is another example of God's super needing our natural to produce the supernatural.

Follow the Instructions

The Lord made a miraculous provision for Elijah after he had boldly declared to King Ahab that there wouldn't be dew or rain until he said so (1 Kgs. 17:1). This produced a severe drought that not only affected the nation, but also Elijah. How would he survive? Then the Lord gave Elijah instructions about His provision.

> *And the word of the* LORD *came unto him, saying, Get thee hence, and turn thee eastward, and hide thyself by the brook Cherith, that* is *before Jordan. And it shall be,* that *thou shalt*

drink of the brook; and I have commanded the ravens to feed thee there.

1 Kings 17:2-4

Notice that the Lord said, "*I **have** commanded the ravens to feed thee there.*" The Lord had already given the command to the ravens to supply Elijah's needs, and since the ravens could fly faster than Elijah could run or walk, the supply was there before he got there. But notice this also, the Lord sent Elijah's supply **there**, to where He told him to go. It was not sent to where he was.

This is profound!

The Lord doesn't send our supply to where we are, but where we are told to go. If Elijah had not gone and done what the Lord told him to do (1 Kgs. 17:5), his supply would have been rotting there by the brook, but he wouldn't have benefited from it.

It's like the quarterback of a football team throwing a pass to the receiver. He doesn't throw the ball to where the receiver is, but he throws it to where he was instructed to go. The Lord always supplies our needs (Phil. 4:19), but are we always in the place we need to be in order to receive? Just as the Lord instructed the ravens to feed Elijah **there**, each of us has a place called there. The problem is that we aren't always there. We often are too much here, waiting on God's provision before we go and do what He tells us to do. It doesn't work that way.

Here's another example. There was a widow who implored Elisha to help meet her needs. Her deceased husband had been one of Elisha's students, and the creditor was demanding her children in lieu of payment.

> *Now there cried a certain woman of the wives of the sons of the prophets unto Elisha, saying, Thy servant my husband is dead; and thou knowest that thy servant did fear the* Lord*: and the creditor is come to take unto him my two sons to be bondmen.*
>
> 2 Kings 4:1

This widow didn't have enough in the natural to meet her needs. She needed a supernatural supply to keep her sons from becoming bond slaves. Yet what did Elisha do? He didn't just meet her needs out of his natural resources. Even if he had enough money to meet her immediate need, that wouldn't have made a lasting difference. This woman needed to trust God for her supply, not Elisha.

So, Elisha wisely pointed her back to the Lord as her source. But the miraculous supply wouldn't just come supernaturally. There were things she needed to do to see God come through.

> *And Elisha said unto her, What shall I do for thee? tell me, what hast thou in the house? And she said, Thine handmaid hath not any thing in the house, save a pot of oil. Then he said, Go, borrow thee vessels abroad of all thy neighbours,* even *empty vessels; borrow not a few. And when thou art come in, thou shalt shut the door upon thee and upon thy sons, and shalt pour out into all those vessels, and thou*

shalt set aside that which is full. So she went from him, and shut the door upon her and upon her sons, who brought the vessels *to her; and she poured out. And it came to pass, when the vessels were full, that she said unto her son, Bring me yet a vessel. And he said unto her,* There is *not a vessel more. And the oil stayed. Then she came and told the man of God. And he said, Go, sell the oil, and pay thy debt, and live thou and thy children of the rest.*

2 Kings 4:2-7

This was absolutely supernatural, but there were natural things this widow had to do in order to receive this supernatural supply. This is evidenced by the fact that when she ran out of vessels, the multiplication of the oil ceased. God's supernatural stopped when she came to the end of what she had done in the natural. There is always a combination of what we have to do in the natural with God's supernatural supply.

This is evidenced in healing too. Naaman the leper came to Elisha to request healing for his leprosy.

So Naaman came with his horses and with his chariot, and stood at the door of the house of Elisha. And Elisha sent a messenger unto him, saying, Go and wash in Jordan seven times, and thy flesh shall come again to thee, and thou shalt be clean. But Naaman was wroth, and went away, and said, Behold, I thought, He will surely come out to me, and stand, and call on the name of the LORD *his God, and strike his hand over the place, and recover the leper.* Are *not Abana and Pharpar, rivers of Damascus, better than all the waters of Israel? may I not wash in them, and be clean? So he turned and went away in a rage.*

2 Kings 5:9-12

Peter told us in 1 Peter 5:5 that God resists the proud but gives grace to the humble. Naaman was a proud man. He was a mighty general of Syria and expected to be treated as such. Elisha didn't even come out to meet him. He just sent a messenger to tell Naaman what to do. This was humiliating to this man, who was used to people bowing to him. He left in anger over Elisha's failure to honor him.

Praise God, the story didn't end there.

> *And his servants came near, and spake unto him, and said, My father,* if *the prophet had bid thee* do some *great thing, wouldest thou not have done* it? *how much rather then, when he saith to thee, Wash, and be clean? Then went he down, and dipped himself seven times in Jordan, according to the saying of the man of God: and his flesh came again like unto the flesh of a little child, and he was clean.*
>
> 2 Kings 5:13-14

Naaman's servants talked him into obeying the instructions that Elisha gave. Naaman went down to the Jordan and dipped seven times in the water. The scriptures clearly state that it was after the seventh time that his flesh became clean.

It was something as simple as dipping in the water seven times that produced Naaman's healing. Actually, it was the fact that he humbled himself and believed the man of God that produced his healing. However, his actions were an essential part of this miracle. If he had not acted on what Elisha told him to do, this healing would not have come. Faith without works is dead, being alone (James 2:17).

On and on I could go with examples of this truth that we have to cooperate with God by doing things in the natural to receive His supernatural results.

What supernatural result are you praying for? Whatever it is, the Lord has already created the supply, but it won't become evident to you until you act on your faith by doing something in the natural.

Do you need salvation? Jesus has already died and paid the debt you owed. It's a done deal, but you won't benefit from it unless you confess with your mouth that Jesus is your Lord (Rom. 10:9). It's God's will for everyone to be saved (2 Pet. 3:9), but not everyone is saved, because they haven't done what He told us to do. You don't get saved because you've done something to earn it. It's a gift that has to be received by believing and acting on your faith (Rom. 6:23 and James 2:17), not a wage to be earned by your good works.

Do you need healing? Jesus has already provided it. First Peter 2:24 says that by the stripes of Jesus, you have already been healed. But that healing won't manifest in your body until you act on your faith.

In John 9, Jesus spit on the ground and made clay of His spittle. Then he put that clay on a blind man's eyes and told him to go to the pool of Siloam and wash. When he did, he was completely healed. This was miraculous, but it wouldn't have happened unless this man had done what Jesus told him to do. The Lord placed His super on what this man did in the natural. The results were supernatural.

This same thing was a part of every miracle Jesus performed. Jesus told ten lepers to go show themselves to the priests and offer the sacrifices the Law commanded a person to do when they had been healed of leprosy. They weren't healed the moment the Lord told them to go, but they were healed as they went (Luke 17:12-19).

The things people did in the natural to receive the supernatural manifestation of God's power were sometimes not obvious, but they were always there. Look at the widow's son that Jesus raised from the dead.

> *And it came to pass the day after, that he went into a city called Nain; and many of his disciples went with him, and much people. Now when he came nigh to the gate of the city, behold, there was a dead man carried out, the only son of his mother, and she was a widow: and much people of the city was with her. And when the Lord saw her, he had compassion on her, and said unto her, Weep not. And he came and touched the bier: and they that bare* him *stood still. And he said, Young man, I say unto thee, Arise. And he that was dead sat up, and began to speak. And he delivered him to his mother.*
>
> Luke 7:11-15

I've had people use this instance to challenge my statement that there has to be something we do in the natural to receive God's supernatural supply. They say,

"What did this dead man do to cooperate with the Lord?" First of all, a statement like that supposes that a dead person has no choice in whether or not they are raised from the dead. I can't say definitively that they do, but you can't say definitively that they don't. I've heard people who were raised from the dead say that the Lord gave them the choice of whether they wanted to come back or not.

Also, notice that Jesus went to the mother of the dead child first and told her not to weep. Why did He do that? If all He wanted to do was to stop her weeping, He could have raised the boy from the dead first. Wouldn't that have stopped her weeping?

Jesus went to the mother first because He needed someone involved in this situation to express some faith. If this mother had not responded to Jesus' instruction positively, I guarantee you there would have been a riot by all the people who were there to support this woman.

I was once kidnapped because a boy who died told everyone that if he died, I would raise him from the dead. The grandmother of this boy was a witch, and she hated me. She once said that if I ever set foot on her property, she would shoot me. When her grandson died, she was afraid I would ruin the funeral by trying to raise him from the dead. So, she arranged to kidnap me and keep me from attending the service. Therefore, I know firsthand that you don't mess with a family's grief by trying to raise someone from the dead.

The lack of resistance to Jesus in this situation shows that this mother must have responded positively to Jesus' words. In Mark 6, Jesus could not—*not would not*—do many mighty works, and it wasn't because of any unbelief on His part. It was the unbelief of the people who had known Him in the flesh for a long time that led them to reject His claims to be the Son of God. They limited the healings that Jesus wanted to do.

So, Jesus approached the mother of this son whom He wanted to raise from the dead. He got a positive response of faith from her in the natural, so that He could put His supernatural power into this situation. That is always the way it works.

I believe the worst doctrine that has invaded the body of Christ is the teaching that nothing happens but what God wills. That is not true. It renders people passive, yet the Bible says we have to resist the devil in order to have him flee from us (James 4:7). The word "resist" means to actively fight against. You can't actively fight against a situation if you think God caused it, or you would be fighting against God.

No! The Lord has conquered death, hell, and the grave, but He delegated that power to us, and if we don't use it, it's not God who is allowing bad things to happen. It's we who are not using our God-given authority who allow whatever the devil wants to do in our lives.

I've seen the Lord do many miraculous things in my life. I've seen my wife and son raised from the dead, blind eyes opened, the lame walk, and the deaf hear. I've had the Lord supply finances so that we can be on worldwide TV and build a multimillion-dollar Bible college campus. I'm certainly not claiming that I'm the one who made all of this happen. It was definitely the Lord and not me who accomplished all these things. But I humbly say that it wouldn't have happened without me. The Lord flows through us. We can't accomplish these things without the Lord, but the Lord can't accomplish anything without us either. You could say He *won't* accomplish anything without us. But the bottom line is, He doesn't move independently of us.

In Acts 10, an angel appeared to Cornelius and told him to send men to Joppa and ask Peter to come and tell him what he had to do to be saved. This angel knew the gospel. He probably knew it better than Peter did. So, why send for Peter to do what that angel could have done? That doesn't seem efficient.

The answer lies in the fact that the Lord didn't give angels the authority to preach the gospel. That's what He commanded us to do (Matt. 10:1-8). It's not the Lord who is letting people enter a Christless eternity. It's the body of Christ, which has failed to take the gospel to the ends of the earth, that has kept people from knowing and believing the truth (Rom. 10:14-17).

Many times, we feel inadequate to share the gospel with others. It's true that we are inadequate. But if we do what we can in the natural, the Lord will add His super to it, and we will get the supernatural results of seeing people born again.

I'm living proof of this. I was an introvert who was so shy that I couldn't talk to a person I didn't already know. Then the Lord called me to preach. There was no way I could do that in just my natural self. I prayed and asked the Lord to change me, but it didn't happen just supernaturally. I had to walk out in front of a crowd by faith and open my mouth before God filled it (Ps. 81:10).

I don't just stand in front of a crowd and pray for the Lord to supernaturally speak through me. I have to talk. If all I did was open my mouth and wait on God to move it and make only His words come out of my mouth, nothing would ever be said. He doesn't control me like that. That's the reason my teaching comes out in Texan. It's me speaking, but I believe the Lord speaks through me.

Take the Limits Off

One of the greatest encounters I ever had with the Lord happened on January 31, 2002. The Lord spoke to me through Psalm 78:41 that I was limiting what He could do through me by my small thinking.

I knew that the Lord wanted me to minister to people all over the world. I was moving in that direction, but at a snail's pace. I made the decision to take the limits off God, and my life and ministry have never been the same. Immediately, I saw the things I was believing for start happening.

At that time, we were only reaching 3% of the U.S. population with my TV program. Today, we reach over two-thirds of the world's population with TV broadcasts in nine languages. Charis Bible College only had just over a hundred students then. Today, we have over 15,000 graduates, with 9,000 students currently enrolled in our 59 schools, located in 22 countries around the world.

The Lord has enabled us to build a Bible college campus worth nearly two hundred million dollars, with plans to more than quadruple that. All of this is the Lord's doing, and it's marvelous in our eyes (Ps. 118:23). I give all the glory to God. But I know that it wouldn't have happened if I had not cooperated with what the Lord was speaking to me.

Today, as I'm writing this, I have one of the biggest opportunities for spreading the gospel that I've ever had presented to me. As I've prayed about whether to take advantage of this, the Lord has said that I'll be blessed if I do it, but I'm still blessed if I don't. If I don't step out, the Lord will find someone else to do it.

I don't want to limit the Lord, so I'm going for it. This is bigger than me, and I know I'm not adequate in myself. But if I do what I can in the natural, God will add His super to it, and we will get supernatural results. The Lord is faithful. What He has done for and through me in the past, He will do again. I've seen it happen many times.

I encourage you to receive this truth that I've been explaining in this little booklet. The Lord has great things in store for every one of us. He has not made any of us just placeholders. His plans for us are good and greater than our plans for ourselves (Jer. 29:11). Most people are shooting at nothing and hitting it every time, but if you will step out in faith and head in the direction the Lord has for your life, He will release His supernatural power to you and through you.

What dream has the Lord put in your heart? Don't just sit there, waiting on the Lord to supply your needs. You've got to do something. It is said that a definition of insanity is to do the same thing repeatedly and yet expect different results.

Learn a lesson from the four lepers:

> *And there were four leprous men at the entering in of the gate: and they said one to another, Why sit we here until we die? If we say, We will enter into the city, then the famine* is *in the city, and we shall die there: and if we sit still here, we die also. Now therefore come, and let us fall unto*

the host of the Syrians: if they save us alive, we shall live; and if they kill us, we shall but die.

2 Kings 7:3-4

The famine had been so severe in the city that people were buying doves' dung for exorbitant prices. They were even cannibalizing their own children (2 Kgs. 6:25-29). And these lepers were even worse off. The people in the city had made them stay outside the city walls because of their disease. If they didn't do something, they were going to die.

But what could they do? If they tried to go into the city, the famine was there, and they were going to die. If they stayed where they were, they were going to die for sure. But if they went out to the Syrian army that surrounded them, they had the possibility that the Syrians might show them mercy. They decided to take the only option that had any possibility of them staying alive. They presented themselves to their enemy, the Syrians.

The result was that when they reached the Syrian camp, the Lord had made the Syrians hear a sound that they interpreted as an army coming against them, and they had fled for their lives. They left their tents, all their goods, and even food that was still cooking on the fires. These lepers went from starving to feasting. They also went from poverty to great riches. They took gold and silver from the tents and expensive garments.

One of the most important things that happened to them was that they went from zeros to heroes. They took the news back to the city that the Syrians had fled and saved everyone from the certain death that seemed to be their fate. Their whole lives and the lives of everyone in the city were changed because they did something in the natural instead of just sitting there, praying for a miracle.

How long are you going to sit there? Till you die?

Prayer is powerful, but just as faith without works is dead (James 2:20), so prayer without action is dead. Don't be like the multitudes who pray for the miraculous intervention of the Lord but won't do anything on their part to bring it to pass. The Lord works through us, not without us.

What's in Your Hand?

When Moses balked at God's instructions to bring the Israelites out of bondage, the Lord asked him what he had in his hand (Ex. 4:2). Moses said it was just a stick. It was the rod he used to herd his sheep. It didn't have any more power than what Moses could produce. If he struck a rock with that rod, it would jar him or possibly break the rod. But when Moses took what was in his hand and laid it down before the Lord, it turned into "the rod of God" (Ex. 4:20).

Now, that rod could split a rock and have millions of gallons of water come out of it to water all the Israelites and their flocks. That same rod turned the Nile into blood and brought all the plagues upon Egypt. It even split the Red Sea and allowed the Jews to pass through it on dry ground while it overcame Pharaoh and all his armies (Ex. 14). It was now God's rod, and it had His supernatural power and authority in it.

When God first commissioned Moses, He told him to lay the rod down on the ground. When he did, it became a serpent, and Moses fled in fear. But God told Moses to pick up the serpent by the tail, and it became a rod again in his hand (Ex. 4:4). Likewise, we need to lay our lives down before the Lord as a living sacrifice (Rom. 12:1). It may seem that if we do so, it will be like facing that serpent, threatening to kill us. But when we pick our life back up by the tail, meaning we are no longer in control because Jesus is seated on the throne of our lives, then it is no longer us living but Christ living through us (Gal. 2:20). Our lives will take on the supernatural power and authority of Jesus with miraculous results.

Do something lest you do nothing. You need to make sure what you do is directed by the Lord and not just your flesh. But I believe inaction is stopping many Christians from accomplishing what the Lord wants to do in their lives. Hebrews 2:15 says that the fear of death is what makes us subject to bondage. There are some things that are worse than death. Living a mediocre life is worse than death. If your life isn't supernatural, it's superficial.

You need to find out what God created you for and then pursue it at all costs. There is a supernatural peace and satisfaction that comes when you are in the center of God's will that you can't experience any other way. It's only after you step out of the boat that you will be able to walk on the water.

My prayer for you is that this has stirred you up. I know the Lord has more for all of us than any of us has ever experienced. If we could possibly tap out all of God's resources, He would just get bigger. He is limitless and wants to do mighty things through you and me.

I'm going for it. How about you?

FURTHER STUDY

If you enjoyed this booklet and would like to learn more about some of the things I've shared, I suggest my teachings:

1. *How to Find, Follow, and Fulfill God's Will*
2. *My Appointment with God*
3. *The Sovereignty of God*
4. *A Place Called There*
5. *The Believer's Authority*

Plus 200,000 hours of free teaching on our website.

These teachings are available for free at **awmi.net**, or they can be purchased at **awmi.net/store**.

Go deeper in your relationship with God by browsing all of Andrew's free teachings.

Receive Jesus as Your Savior

Choosing to receive Jesus Christ as your Lord and Savior is the most important decision you'll ever make!

God's Word promises, "*That if thou shalt confess with thy mouth the Lord Jesus, and shalt believe in thine heart that God hath raised him from the dead, thou shalt be saved. For with the heart man believeth unto righteousness; and with the mouth confession is made unto salvation*" (Rom. 10:9–10). "*For whosoever shall call upon the name of the Lord shall be saved*" (Rom. 10:13). By His grace, God has already done everything to provide salvation. Your part is simply to believe and receive.

Pray out loud: "Jesus, I acknowledge that I've sinned and need to receive what you did for the forgiveness of my sins. I confess that You are my Lord and Savior. I believe in my heart that God raised You from the dead. By faith in Your Word, I receive salvation now. Thank You for saving me."

The very moment you commit your life to Jesus Christ, the truth of His Word instantly comes to pass in your spirit. Now that you're born again, there's a brand-new you!

Please contact us and let us know that you've prayed to receive Jesus as your Savior. We'd like to send you some free materials to help you on your new journey. Call our Helpline: **719-635-1111** (available 24 hours a day, seven days a week) to speak to a staff member who is here to help you understand and grow in your new relationship with the Lord.

Welcome to your new life!

Receive the Holy Spirit

As His child, your loving heavenly Father wants to give you the supernatural power you need to live a new life. *"For every one that asketh receiveth; and he that seeketh findeth; and to him that knocketh it shall be opened... how much more shall* your *heavenly Father give the Holy Spirit to them that ask him?"* (Luke 11:10–13).

All you have to do is ask, believe, and receive! Pray this: "Father, I recognize my need for Your power to live a new life. Please fill me with Your Holy Spirit. By faith, I receive it right now. Thank You for baptizing me. Holy Spirit, You are welcome in my life."

Some syllables from a language you don't recognize will rise up from your heart to your mouth (1 Cor. 14:14). As you speak them out loud by faith, you're releasing God's power from within and building yourself up in the spirit (1 Cor. 14:4). You can do this whenever and wherever you like.

It doesn't really matter whether you felt anything or not when you prayed to receive the Lord and His Spirit. If you believed in your heart that you received, then God's Word promises you did. *"Therefore I say unto you, What things soever ye desire, when ye pray, believe that ye receive* them, *and ye shall have* them" (Mark 11:24). God always honors His Word—believe it!

We would like to rejoice with you, pray with you, and answer any questions to help you understand more fully what has taken place in your life!

Please contact us to let us know that you've prayed to be filled with the Holy Spirit and to request the book *The New You & the Holy Spirit*. This book will explain in more detail about the benefits of being filled with the Holy Spirit and speaking in tongues. Call our Helpline: **719-635-1111** (available 24 hours a day, seven days a week).

Call for Prayer

If you need prayer for any reason, you can call our Helpline, 24 hours a day, seven days a week at **719-635-1111**. A trained prayer minister will answer your call and pray with you.

Every day, we receive testimonies of healings and other miracles from our Helpline, and we are ministering God's nearly-too-good-to-be-true message of the Gospel to more people than ever. So, I encourage you to call today!

About the Author

Andrew Wommack's life was forever changed the moment he encountered the supernatural love of God on March 23, 1968. As a renowned Bible teacher and author, Andrew has made it his mission to change the way the world sees God.

Andrew's vision is to go as far and deep with the Gospel as possible. His message goes far through the *Gospel Truth* television program, which is available to over half the world's population. The message goes deep through discipleship at Charis Bible College, headquartered in Woodland Park, Colorado. Founded in 1994, Charis has campuses across the United States and around the globe.

Andrew also has an extensive library of teaching materials in print, audio, and video. More than 200,000 hours of free teachings can be accessed at **awmi.net**.

Contact Information

Andrew Wommack Ministries, Inc.

PO Box 3333
Colorado Springs, CO 80934-3333
info@awmi.net
awmi.net

Helpline: 719-635-1111 (available 24/7)

Charis Bible College

info@charisbiblecollege.org
844-360-9577
CharisBibleCollege.org

For international offices
visit **awmi.net/contact-us**.

Connect with us on social media.

Andrew Wommack's *Living Commentary* digital study Bible is a user-friendly, downloadable program. It's like reading the Bible with Andrew at your side, sharing his revelation with you verse by verse.

Main features:

- Bible study software with a grace-and-faith perspective
- Over 27,000 notes by Andrew on verses from Genesis through Revelation
- *Adam Clarke's Commentary on the Bible*
- *Albert Barnes' Notes on the Whole Bible*
- *Matthew Henry's Concise Commentary*
- 12 Bible versions
- 3 optional premium translation add-ons: *New Living Translation*, *New International Version*, and *The Message* (additional purchase of $9.99 each)
- 2 concordances: *Englishman's Concordance* and *Strong's Concordance*
- 2 dictionaries: *Collaborative International Dictionary* and *Holman's Dictionary*
- Atlas with biblical maps
- Bible and *Living Commentary* statistics
- Quick navigation, including history of verses
- Robust search capabilities (for the Bible and Andrew's notes)
- "Living" (i.e., constantly updated and expanding)
- Ability to create personal notes
- Accessible online and offline

Whether you're new to studying the Bible or a seasoned Bible scholar, you'll gain a deeper revelation of the Word from a grace-and-faith perspective.

Purchase Andrew's *Living Commentary* today at **awmi.net/living** and grow in the Word with Andrew.

Item code: 8350

ANDREW WOMMACK MINISTRIES

www.ingramcontent.com/pod-product-compliance
Lightning Source LLC
LaVergne TN
LVHW012334100826
845148LV00017B/2633

* 9 7 8 1 5 9 5 4 8 7 9 6 4 *